SELL YOUR VISION

You have been given a wonderful opportunity. Are you going to recognize it, seize upon it, and live out your dreams, or be one of the many poor souls who wonder what might have been? The choice is yours and yours alone. I wish each of you nothing but the best.

—Don Green,
Executive Director of
The Napoleon Hill Foundation

SELL YOUR VISION

The Golden Rules *for*
Long-term Success *and*
Guaranteed Satisfaction

Napoleon Hill

Published and distributed by:
SOUND WISDOM
P.O. Box 310
Shippensburg, PA 17257-0310
717-530-2122

info@soundwisdom.com

www.soundwisdom.com

While efforts have been made to verify information contained in this publication, neither the author nor the publisher assumes any responsibility for errors, inaccuracies, or omissions. While this publication is chock-full of useful, practical information; it is not intended to be legal or accounting advice. All readers are advised to seek competent lawyers and accountants to follow laws and regulations that may apply to specific situations. The reader of this publication assumes responsibility for the use of the information. The author and publisher assume no responsibility or liability whatsoever on the behalf of the reader of this publication.

ISBN 13 TP: 978-1-64095-495-3

ISBN 13 eBook: 978-1-64095-496-0

For Worldwide Distribution, Printed in the U.S.A.

1 2 3 4 5 6 7 8 / 28 27 26 25 24

CONTENTS

CONTENTS

INTRODUCTION

Napoleon Hill is the author of *Think and Grow Rich*, *Master Key to Riches,* and other best-selling books. He is also the creator of the American Philosophy of Individual Achievement. His discussion on "going the extra mile" has made hundreds of thousands of wealthy men and women worldwide who have taken the time to put his wisdom into practice in their lives.

Every person needs a philosophy of life and in Dr. Hill's books you will find the principles to guide you and sustain you in whatever work you have chosen. His philosophy does not conflict in any way with your religion or your political beliefs—but rather augments and amplifies them.

Although written a few decades ago, the wisdom, advice, humor, and proven-successful strategies are just as relevant now than they were then—in fact, even more so.

In this mini but mighty book, Napoleon Hill presents the nuts and bolts of his philosophy of success that include: Going the Extra Mile, developing a Positive Mental Attitude, choosing to Understand Yourself and Others, generating Harmonious Health, and Finishing Unfinished Business—each topic vital when aiming for a life of success and happiness. Launching Chapter 1 in this slice of his philosophy is Dr. Hill's personal Success Creed, which sets the tone for the remainder of the book filled with profitable insight and practical ways to secure your desired future.

For example, *Going the Extra Mile* is a principle that offers you five life-enhancing benefits: 1) receive compensation in excess of the value of the service rendered; 2) achieve greater strength of character; 3) increased positive mental attitude; 4) experience an increase in self-reliance, personal initiative, and enthusiasm; 5) assurance of always having employment. This principle and others are explained, including how to get a job and how to make a sale.

Napoleon Hill shares with you what he learned along the way in life and tells you how to use his philosophy to attain success, but not merely financial success. Napoleon Hill's nuts and bolts tool kit helps you to also attain joy, peace of mind, important relationships, and a life-time of beneficial habits—as well as monetary wealth.

To stimulate ideas, formulate plans, and enforce the principles, "noodling" questions have been included at the conclusion of each chapter. These prompts were designed to aid in affecting your advancement toward achieving your goals.

We at the Napoleon Hill Foundation hope this mini-book will inspire you to look into Napoleon Hill's original books that delve more deeply into matters of personal achievement, helping you reach that point in life when all of your plans have been fulfilled and you achieve every goal.

Don M. Green
Chief Executive Officer and Executive Director
Napoleon Hill Foundation

1

MY
SUCCESS
CREED

At the end of a hard day's work, I turned to my type-writer one day and typed at the top, "My Success Creed." Followed by:

Realizing that service is all I have to give in return for the fortune I hope to accumulate, I hereby adopt this simple creed:

- *I will render more service and better service than I am paid to render,* because this will create keen competition for my services and enable me to command the top-notch price for my work. All around me I see evidences of people who failed because they lacked self-control; therefore, I will impose a discipline upon myself that will enable me always to refrain from doing or saying anything that will turn neutral acquaintances or friends into enemies.

- *I will listen* more and talk less; I will think more carefully before I speak; I will be more friendly and less hostile toward all whom I meet.

- *I will go out of my way* to render acts of kindness with no thought of being paid except through the happiness that this procedure will bring me.

- *I will make friends* because of my willingness to be friendly.

- *I will do away with intolerance, bias, prejudice, hatred, and anger* because these negative qualities do not attract to me the sort of people with whom I wish to ally myself.

- *I will do my best to practice the Golden Rule* as well as preach it, because I realize that I will eventually reap what I sow.

This would not be a poor creed to copy and hang on the walls of your room, or in the place where you work. It would not be a poor creed to adopt as your own.

A DOLLAR A MINUTE

In addition to my success creed, now I give you the benefit of one of the most interesting and successful campaigns I ever created.

First of all, I selected a list of twenty-five presidents of various corporations where I preferred to secure employment. This list of twenty-five became my mailing list, so to speak, and this is the manner in which I went at them, step by step.

The first day the following telegram was sent to each of the twenty-five as my first approach:

I will listen more and talk less; I will think more carefully before I speak.

> In today's mail I am sending you an important
> installment of a message that will be delivered
> to you a little at a time each day during the next
> week. After you have read the last word of the
> last installment of this message, I will send you
> my check for a dollar a minute for the time you
> have spent reading the message if you do not
> say that it concerns a subject in which you are
> vitally interested.

This telegram was sent on Monday morning. Its object
was to appeal to the curiosity of the recipient, and at the
same time prove that the sender was resourceful, imag-
inative, and somewhat out of the ordinary in making an
approach.

The same day that the telegram was sent the following
letter was mailed by Special Delivery:

> In all your business experience I hazard the
> guess that you never thought it good business
> to reach a decision until all available facts were
> before you. The position you hold is strong evi-
> dence that you have good judgment; that you
> know the difference between people who have
> initiative and those who have not; and that
> you do not consider your time wasted when

listening to a salesman who has come to sell you something that you want and need.

I have something that you need and I am sure you will want it when you find out what it is and what it can do for you. Tomorrow I will begin describing the machine which I have for sale. My letter will come in this same sort of approach, under a Special Delivery stamp. Therefore, will you please have it delivered to you immediately upon its arrival? I know you will be interested in its contents.

Very Cordially.

The second day I sent the following letter:

The machine about which I wrote you yesterday is not exactly what one might call a new invention, yet there is not another one like it in all the world. This machine will practically relieve you of unnecessary detail. It will produce harmony among the employees around your office, and this will extend itself into your plant. This machine will cause the employees of your office to develop greater efficiency and work in smoother harmony with one another and with you. It will cause them to develop the following philosophy and, to some extent at least, practice it:

First, it will cause them to do more and better work than they are paid to do, because it will enable them to benefit by your self-interest and sound business judgment, in that you will be sure to respond in an appropriate manner. You will do so because you will want to encourage the rendering of such service.

Second, this machine will radiate good cheer around your office and cause all of the employees to understand the truth in the statement that whatever a man sows that shall he also reap. The machine will act as an incentive to all within its range to sow nothing in the way of poor service because of their unwillingness to reap a crop of corresponding remuneration.

More about this machine tomorrow.

Very cordially.

The third day the following letter was sent to each of the twenty-five:

What would such a machine as the one described in my letter yesterday be worth to a corporation such as the one you are the directing head?

Would you rent such a machine on a basis that would cost you only in proportion to what it actually earned for you in increased efficiency, extending all the way from your own desk down to the humblest laborer in your employ?

Such machines cannot be valued entirely in the dollars they earn or save, because the peace of mind they would create is worth more than the money they would save.

More tomorrow.

Very cordially.

The fourth day this letter was sent to each of the twenty-five:

Robert Fulton once sought an interview with Napoleon. He went there to offer the great general the use of his steamboat invention. Napoleon had long yearned for some means of crossing the English Channel hurriedly so he could attack the British by surprise and defeat them. Fulton's invention would have turned the trick, but, when a messenger announced Fulton and told Napoleon what he had come for and what he claimed for his invention,

Napoleon replied, "What! Sail a boat against the wind? It can't be done."

You now know, of course, what a fool Napoleon made of himself in passing judgment before evidence had been submitted. Of course, men in this day and time are not so foolish; at least men who are in positions such as the one you hold. They are always on the alert for someone with an idea, even a simple idea that will help them develop greater efficiency in their work, more loyalty in their coworkers and greater peace of mind for themselves.

Of course, YOU will not turn me away when I come to show you the machine about which I have written you.

Very cordially.

On the fifth day the following letter was sent to each of the twenty-five:

Tomorrow I will write you the last of this series of little messages concerning a machine which I wish to rent to you for a very reasonable rental fee that is based upon a very fair and equitable scale.

In the meantime, I wish to apologize for stringing my message out day by day, thus making it somewhat annoying to you to keep up with the trend of thought. I have done this for only one reason, namely: I have offered this machine to twenty-four others who, like yourself, hold responsible positions with big corporations.

Some of the twenty-five will become impatient and like Napoleon, whose name I share, will throw my letters in the wastebasket and think that "It can't be done." I hope you will not be one of the unfortunate ones who will make this mistake. But if you are, it will be to my advantage to find this out before I rent you the machine.

Very cordially.

On the sixth day the following letter was sent:

Today I have come with my last message concerning the machine described in my first letter. I am ready, when you have read the last word of this letter, to show the machine and let you see it perform, or hand you my check for your time at the rate of a dollar a minute, which is all I can afford to pay you, even though you may be worth more.

The machine I have referenced is the most remarkable sort of machine in all the world. God made it. What He made it for I do not know, but I strongly suspect that He planned for it to be as efficient as possible, and to be constructive and cooperative. I suspect He never planned that this machine would be used to tear down, undermine, or destroy.

The machine I reference reposes in my head. It is called, for want of a better name, a brain. It can and will perform all that was promised in previous letters. It can and will create harmony among your employees. It can and will render more service and better service than you actually pay for or expect. It can and will relieve you of much of your detail; but you will never know whether I speak the truth or not until you have tried this human machine.

It will cost you nothing to try it. I will present it at your office for preliminary examination any time you say. I will put it into operation for you for one month; and if at the end of the month the chances for it doing all that I claim for it seem promising, you may retain it by paying a rental of $150 a month. On the other hand, you may relieve it of duty and there will be no ill feelings and no expense.

Very cordially.

This series brought the most remarkable collection of answers you ever saw. Twelve of the men offered me the position I sought, without the formality of an interview. Five of them offered me different positions, one of them offering me the position of sales and advertising manager. Eight of them had no opening at the time but requested me to keep them informed of my whereabouts as they wished to communicate with me later. Within six months from that time four of these eight had offered me positions, one of them at a higher salary than I had asked for my services.

If you will analyze these letters carefully, you will see that the main appeal was in the fact that I was willing to show a sample of my goods before collecting for them, and that the wording of the letters showed I had the right notion about rendering service generally. The unusual appeal through six letters and a telegram was for the purpose of securing attention by arousing curiosity—*and it worked!*

COOL CUCUMBER OR HOT HEAD

Cool Cucumber

A few weeks ago, I went into the office of a business in which I am the silent owner, and while waiting to see the

I will make friends because of my willingness to be friendly.

president of the company I asked the young lady at the stenographer's desk if I might use the telephone to communicate with my own office for a moment.

She replied, "Why, certainly." Just then the man whom I had come to see came out to greet me. The stenographer took in the situation, saw that I was about to be ushered inside, and therefore asked if I would like to give her the number I wanted and the name of the person to whom I wished to speak so she could attend to the call for me.

Mind you, she did not have to be requested to render this service. She used initiative and rendered the service voluntarily. Not only did she render service but service of the highest order by not only asking for the telephone number, but requested the name of the person, thus saving me the time and annoyance of attending to the details myself.

Had the young lady known I owned the company for which she was working, I should have thought only so much of her unusual service. But she had not the slightest inkling that she was rendering this service to the man who was paying her salary. Her attitude was so unusual that immediately I began to plan ways and means of attaching her to my personal staff. I arranged with her immediate superior to release her from the position she was holding, and she is now one of my most efficient secretaries. The position sought her, as you can plainly see.

That is not all; she could get any one of half a dozen other good jobs tomorrow if she desired to leave my employ. She automatically applies this rule of rendering more service and better service than she is actually paid to deliver, no matter what she may be doing—and this practice always leads to greater and more profitable responsibilities.

Hot Head

On the other side of the coin, I watched the unusual process of a man "firing himself." This man approached me for a position. He made a fine appearance. He talked well. He impressed me favorably.

But I put him to the test, to find out what sort of appearance he would make on the firing line of business instead of in the reception rooms of my office. I wanted to see what he would do in action, under the load of business responsibilities. I gave him a conditional tryout. Without telling him why I was doing so, I had his desk placed in my private office where I could watch every move he made, without disconcerting him.

The first three days he got along very well because not much work was assigned to him. Yet I felt reasonably sure there was something about this fellow beneath the surface that would explain why he had reached middle age without having succeeded in anchoring himself to anything of permanence. I felt sure, also, that his finely polished surface would render it impossible for me to find out what his weakness was without seeing him face trying, exasperating experiences that would make him angry—so I planned a little trap and arranged for him to be angered.

The plan worked well. He picked up the telephone and, because the operator did not give him his number instantly, he jammed the receiver down so hard that he broke it into pieces, and swore at her viciously!

Because of that one demonstration, in less than twenty-four hours I had found out this man's entire life story; it was a pathetic one. He had been connected with some of the biggest and best-known concerns in America, in positions of responsibility. Yet in every instance, he had lost out because he had not exercised self-control. At one time he was fairly well off financially, but he lost every dollar. Today, he is a failure, at an age when he can ill afford to be on the defensive side of life. He could not control his dollars because he would not control himself.

Had he shown the same coolness under the responsibilities of a position that he did when he was seeking one and trying to sell his services, he would today be the business manager of one of my enterprises, in the position for which I had him scheduled before he "fired himself." Would anyone deny that he actually discharged himself?

What I would make plain is that this principle works in exactly the same manner when the stenographer renders more service and better service than she is paid to render, or when the bookkeeper or the foreman or the trucker or the general manager of the works does the same.

I want to show you how to sell your services and how to keep them sold, no matter what your life work may be. Therefore, I feel more than justified in repeating again and again this crucial, life-changing *principle of rendering service that is better in quality and greater in quantity than you contract to deliver.*

POINTS TO PONDER

1. What point or points in "The Success Creed" most resonated with you? Have you been living by a similar yet unwritten creed?

2. Are these attributes ones you realize have the potential to make you a better manager, employee, spouse, parent, student—all round better person? Which one will you strive to live first?

3. What clever and unusual approach to sales or employment came to mind while reading this six-letter scenario?

4. Using today's various means of communication, how can you wisely connect with 15-20 people who can help you reach your objective of selling a service, product, yourself?

5. If seeking a job, how "sold" are you on the promise of working for no compensation for a month? A week?

6. Have you ever fired yourself or lost a sale because of your lack of self-control? Would you describe yourself as a hot head or a cool cucumber?

7. Has anger caused you to lose a sale, a job, a relationship? What steps can you take to cool your emotions no matter the circumstance?

2

FORTUNES DEPEND ON...

B efore we start, know that I intend to go much farther than telling you "how to get a job" or "how to sell a product." We are going to the very bottom of the subject to uncover the chief fundamental principles through which you may not only get "a" job, but you may get "the" job for which you are best suited. This discovery also involves selling, yourself and whatever product or service you wish to sell.

We will go still deeper into this worldwide important subject and show you how to fill the position satisfactorily and profitably after you get it—as well as maintain and retain your sales.

The great gateway to fame and fortune through which all who succeed must pass might properly be labeled "Personal Service!" All that you have or ever will have to give in return for the fortune which you hope to accumulate is personal services!

Ponder over this and you will unconsciously lay the foundation for the point I wish to make, namely, that the size of that *fortune will depend, not on what you wish it to be, but on the quality and quantity of service you render the world!*

PLEASE THE PURCHASER

It would be impossible to give you a definite rule to follow that would apply in all cases, but you may put it down as an essential requirement that *success will never crown your efforts in any undertaking unless you please the purchaser of your services.* Your services or product may be satisfactory in both quality and quantity, but this is not enough—your method of rendering or offering must actually please the purchaser!

I am writing almost within the shadow of one of the largest and best-known retail merchandise establishments in the world, Marshall Field & Company. That great business was built on just one simple idea: *"Every customer must go away from the store satisfied."* Profits are secondary when it comes to providing goods and service that actually pleases the buyer and makes him or her want to come back again.

I had lunch with Mr. McKinley, Vice President of Marshall Field & Company. He said that one of the biggest problems confronting them was that of training their employees to reflect this spirit of service in every transaction, large or small. Marshall Field saw clearly, without anyone to suggest it to him, the commercial value of pleasing the buyer. Yet the big task in keeping the Marshall Field spirit alive in those who now manage the Field store is to get the 3,000 employees to absorb the Field idea of service!

I do not presume to be able to tell you *how* to please those whom you serve and to whom you are selling your services or products because you are the best judge of that—but I do tell you to *seek until you find the right method and then make use of it to please each and every person!*

It is an interesting experience and a rare privilege to study the officials of the Marshall Field Store at close range. In these people you may find one principle in common which we could all well afford to copy—the principle of "service."

THE PRINCIPLE OF SERVICE

Herein lies the secret of the success of the Field business, which endures even though the founder has been dead many years. The principle of service, if rightly administered, never dies! Through application of this principle you may insert yourself in the hearts of people, where the principles for which you stand will live long after your body has gone back to dust.

You will succeed only by selling satisfactory service by pleasing those who purchase your services. Keep this ever in mind and the roadway of satisfactory service will open to you when you need it!

If I have seemed to dwell at length on this prelude on "service," know that I am justified by the importance of the subject.

Fortune will depend, not on what you wish it to be, but on the quality and quantity of service you render the world!

This brings us to a suitable point to present a complete chart of the chief factors that enter into the sale of personal services and products of every nature whatsoever. My intention is that this chart is so thorough and yet so simple that anyone may make immediate application of it.

SELLING YOUR PERSONAL SERVICES AND/OR PRODUCTS

The first factor for consideration in seeking employment is the selection of the right position, in a line of work you are best fitted by nature, training, inclination, and experience. The position you select should be *the one you like best!* From this point on we shall go on the assumption that you have selected the right vocation, career.

The same is true for selling a product. Potential buyers will notice if you are trying to sell them something that you are not sold on yourself.

The following is a complete analysis chart covering all of the important subjects connected with the sale of personal services and/or products:

Analysis of Your Product

Before you proceed to offer your services for sale, take inventory to arrive at the following facts as a basis for offering your services:

- What sort of services/products have you to market?

- What is the value of the services/ products you have to offer?

- Who is the most available purchaser?

You will not have even a starting point until you have accurately organized this information.

Service You Render

- Quality must be right.

- Quantity must be right.

- Your method of rendering it must be satisfactory to the purchaser.

Cause and Effect

- The service/product you render is cause.

- The pay you receive is effect.

- If the "effect" is not satisfactory, examine "cause" and you will find the reason.

Opportunity to Display Sample of Your "Goods"

- Getting a job is a mere preliminary or chance to show a small sample of the sort of service you can render. The actual procuring of the job is of only secondary importance.

- Displaying your goods or products is equally important—putting each in the best presentation possible, always with the customer in mind.

Methods of Securing Position or Presenting Product

- Application in person.

- Application by letter.

- Advertisement in newspapers.

- Application through employment agencies.

- Attracting employers or purchasers to you through unusually satisfactory services rendered. If you offer your services or products in person, carefully guard your personal appearance. If you apply by letter it will be necessary for you to properly construct that letter and guard its "personal appearance" as carefully as you would your own if you were applying in person.

Gather and Organize Data Concerning the Position, Firm, or Individual

- Gather all available facts concerning the position you wish to secure, or all information for the products you wish to sell.

- Gather all information concerning the firm or individual, the nature of the business, and particularly all who would gain from a sales presentation, showing you to be fully qualified to fill the position before you actually apply for it—or qualified to sell and service the product. All this data should be fully assimilated, organized, and correlated, thereby preparing yourself to show just where and how you would fit into the position you seek, or how the product would greatly benefit the purchaser.

Qualities to Make Your Services or Products Desirable and Sought After

- Willingness on your part—not only a "willingness" but an intense desire—to do more work than you are paid for.

- Intense interest and boundless enthusiasm in your work to perform.

- Pleasing personality: cheerfulness, optimism, courage.

- Self-confidence.

- Initiative: the habit of seeing and actually performing more work than the job you fill requires, without being told to do so.

- Action: habit of doing your work promptly.

- Power of analysis: ability to see more, hear more, and know more about your job or product and the business than those around you. This includes the ability to gather, organize, classify, and correlate all relevant facts concerning your every task and responsibility.

- Willingness to and actual practice of reaching outside the immediate sphere of your own duties and assuming more responsibilities and commitment.

- Leadership: the ability to get others to perform work willingly and gladly, with cheerfulness, not merely because they are afraid not to do so, but because they wish to do so. The ability to command the respect and confidence of associate workers, whether in a higher or lower position.

- Loyalty: as a matter of course.

- Persistence: not only the ability but the actual practice of properly finishing all that you start.

- Concentration: the ability to keep your mind focused on a task or sale until completed.

Let me give you a few brief suggestions as to the proper use of this chart. Probably the most satisfactory method to follow is this:

1. Write your name at the top of a sheet of paper and analyze your "product"—the services you wish to market under the heading PRODUCT ANALYSIS. Write out a complete description of the sort of services you have to market, what you believe the value of these services to be, and a list of names of the most available and desirable employers. This will give you a splendid starting point, and everything must have a beginning.

2. Under the heading SERVICE YOU RENDER, write out a complete description of what you believe to be the quality of your services, the quantity you intend to deliver to the prospective employer, and the method or "spirit" in which you intend to deliver this service.

3. Under the heading CAUSE AND EFFECT, write out, in your own words, your understanding of the principle that "the service you render is cause, while the pay you receive is effect." This is a principle you will do well to thoroughly understand and apply.

There is a cause for every effect!

It is not reasonable, therefore, to suppose that there is a cause for unsatisfactory compensation for personal services rendered. The cause may be traceable to the person who renders the services, or it may be traced to the purchaser, who in some instances is selfish and unfair. In the majority of cases, however, you will find the cause connected with one or all of the following:

1. The *quality* of services rendered is
    unsatisfactory.

2. The *quantity* of services rendered is
    unsatisfactory.

3. The *manner* in which services are rendered
    is unsatisfactory.

If you find the trouble here, you will readily see that only the seller can eliminate.

Before blaming the purchaser of your services for your lean pay envelope it is well to analyze yourself by applying this formula and ascertaining whether or not you are at fault. If you are not at fault—if the quality of your services is A-1, the quantity is abundant and the manner in which you are rendering the service is highly satisfactory and still the pay envelope is not sufficient—there are only two conclusions at which to arrive: 1) you are a poor salesman, or 2) the purchaser of your services is unjust and unfair.

If your salesmanship is poor you can improve it, and if the purchaser of your services is unjust or short sighted and unfair with you, find another purchaser!

Failure to comply with one or the other of these suggestions is the chief reason why men and women of ability go through life chained to mediocre positions, or worse, as complete failures without a position!

People will know if you are trying to sell them something that you are not sold on yourself.

4. Under the heading OPPORTUNITY TO DISPLAY YOUR GOODS, write out your understanding, in your own words, that a job or a sale is nothing more than a beginning point—a chance to "deliver the goods," so to speak. The biggest job in the world is nothing more than a mere "chance" to sell your services or product as long as you please your purchaser.

The reason so few people have big jobs is due very largely to the fact that so few people regard their jobs as an "opportunity." Nearly every job is a "big job in the making." Nearly every job has the potentialities of a big job, if properly developed.

5. Under the heading METHODS FOR SECURING POSITION, write down all the available channels through which you intend to seek employment, unless, of course, you merely wish to market your services to better advantage with your present employer, which is often the best thing to do.

If you apply or approach in person, you should be mindful of your personal appearance. This applies to the person seeking a position as bricklayer as much as it does to the person seeking an executive or clerical position in an office—and a person selling farm equipment or corporate insurance. Slovenliness and an unsightly appearance always carry a negative effect that makes it hard to sell his or herself to best advantage. In many arenas, no one would even be considered who did not have a well-kept personal appearance.

If there is ever a time when you should look your best, it is when you are going to be interviewed for a position or presenting a sales pitch. Not only will you create a favorable impression in the purchaser's mind, but also because of the additional courage and self-confidence it will give you! Clean and well-pressed clothes, carefully brushed hair, clean finger nails, a smile, and a quick, reassuring, springy step that goes with this look, are all important assets you cannot afford to be without!

In offering your services by letter, be sure to send out your little personal messenger dressed in the best of "clothes"—stationary! The first appearance of your letter may determine its fate, just as the first glance at a person who applies in person may determine his or her fate. There is only one chance to make a first impression! Of course, good stationary alone will not suffice. It merely secures for your letter serious attention.

Personally, if I were applying for a position, I would prefer to make use of both the letter and personal interview. I would select my prospective employer or customer, and through one or more carefully written letters I would endeavor to make him feel that he wanted to see me in person. I would avoid, if possible, bringing him to a point where he could say "no" before he had seen me in person. The purpose of the letter or letters would be entirely to make the prospect feel that he wanted to talk to me. I would construct my letters so he would request me to come and see him.

6. GATHER AND ORGANIZE ALL DATA is a good way to begin such a campaign. Gather information and facts available concerning the prospect's business in general, and the position you desire to fill, in particular! When selling a product, gather information regarding how your product will enhance the person's goals or the business's mission.

I would not say a word about a position, but instead move right ahead and submit some concrete suggestions that he could make use of in connection with his business, whether he employed me or not. In other words, I would actually attach myself to his working staff, without pay, and without asking his permission. This unusual procedure gains "favorable attention" for me, and from this point on negotiations would be easy!

This last-mentioned method of attracting employers to you through unusually satisfactory services rendered needs a little comment. While this method has been mentioned last, it is nevertheless the most important of all those mentioned, to all except those who are applying for their first position. This is so for the reason that in every position there are undeveloped possibilities that one may develop by rendering the right sort of service.

Fortunate is the person who looks upon his or her position as an opportunity to attract favorable attention by rendering unusually satisfactory service! Such a person is bound to succeed; if not in a present position, then in a bigger and better one somewhere else.

No lawyer of reputation would think of going into court with a case until he or she had gathered every available fact and every scintilla of information concerning it. They would organize these facts and be prepared to present them to the court in logical sequence.

You must be prepared to do the same when you present yourself for employment or desire to make a sale.

7. This brings us to the last subject: QUALITIES THAT MAKE YOUR SERVICES DESIRABLE—EVEN SOUGHT AFTER. No argument need be advanced to prove that all the qualities mentioned under the chart's heading are desirable to develop, but the question is, how may these qualities be developed in a person who does not already possess them?

Before answering this question, it is necessary to briefly mention a principle through the operation of which all of these qualities and others as well may be quickly developed—auto-suggestion.

Auto-suggestion means simply suggestions we make to ourselves. It is surprising, however, to know how few people actually understand the possibilities of achievement through the use of auto-suggestion. It is not my intention to enter into any lengthy argument as to the merits of auto-suggestion. I know that it has worked wonders in my own life and I have seen it work wonders in the lives of others—wonders which, in many respects, seemed as miraculous as anything that happened in the biblical days of two thousand years ago!

In digressing from the subject of how to sell your services, to briefly discuss the method through which you may develop those desirable positive qualities, I am taking it for granted that you wish to be thorough—that you want all the available information you can get, not only on the secondary question of securing an immediate job or making a sale, but also on the more important subject of ascertaining how to build your job or sale into a bigger and more profitable one.

To give you this information I must at least discuss briefly the subject of auto-suggestion, for it will be through application of this principle that you will cultivate the qualities necessary in filling a big position.

It has been proved by the world's most able scientists and psychologists that every thought or idea placed in the human mind and systematically held there, through concentration, has a tendency to reproduce itself in bodily, muscular action.

For example, if you think of fear constantly, you will be afraid and your bodily actions will be directed accordingly. On the other hand, if you think of courage, your bodily actions will be courageous. If you hate another person, that person will likely hate you, because you cannot think hate and keep from showing it in one way or another, through bodily action or facial expression.

The greatest of all philosophers and teachers probably had in mind the principles of auto-suggestion when He said, "Whatsoever ye soweth that shall ye also reap!" If you will take my word for it, I will assure you that I have experimented with this principle until I know that it is as immutable as is the law of gravity.

"Is it possible," I hear you say, "that by simply placing in my mind the thoughts I would like to see reproduced in physical reality, I can accomplish such remarkable results?"

And I answer, "Not only is this possible, but it is unavoidable!"

This being true, you can readily see how important it is to make use of the principle of auto-suggestion. The procedure is very simple. Probably that is why so few people have had enough faith in it to make a more organized application of it.

Let us make use of this principle in developing a list of desirable qualities. Two examples follow:

1. *From this day on I will cheerfully perform more work than I am paid to perform, never complaining, because I know that in time this habit will be appreciated by my employers and I will be paid accordingly.*

One of the remarkable things about auto-suggestion is the fact that the very minute you write out this sentence, if you sincerely intend to do what you have pledged, you will find your every action directed toward carrying out your pledge!

Then, take the next quality that you desire to develop, and write it out as follows:

> **2.** *I love my work, and from this day on I will be ever alert for opportunities to do better work and more of it. I am enthusiastic about and intensely interested in my work, and I will do everything in my power to perform it more satisfactorily than any other person could.*

Go right down the list until you have written out every quality you intend to develop, in every case stating, in your own words, just what you are going to do to develop that quality. When the list is complete, commit it to memory by reading it aloud several times a day.

Auto-suggestion is most effective when it is followed by action as well as mere affirmations or wishes. The words you use are not so important as long as they represent definite positive ideas or thoughts. Your affirmations must not be vague, however; because if they are, the results will also be vague.

This is all there is to the principle of auto-suggestion; at least all that I can tell you about. If you do not apply this principle, it will not benefit you. It works no miracles without your hearty and persistent cooperation! But with these, it will give you the surprise of your life and place you wherever you wish to be!

POINTS TO PONDER

1. Do you believe that *the size of your fortune depends not on what you wish it to be, but on the quality and quantity of service or product you offer the world?* Explain your answer.

2. Is pleasing every purchaser (of services or products) a reasonable goal to aspire to accomplish? What circumstances may exist that would preclude that outcome?

3. Was the analysis chart helpful? Did it cover all the important subjects connected with the sale of personal services and/or products? What more could you add to the chart? What wasn't helpful?

4. Do you see every job and/or sale as an opportunity? Write your thoughts about how seeing opportunity opens yourself to possibilities—venture into exceptional experiences regarding your potential.

5. "Whatsoever ye soweth that shall ye also reap!" Is the expression, "What goes around comes around" similar in concept as the sower/reaper quotation? How do both relate to your philosophy of life?

6. How will you make auto-suggestion work for you? Will you take advantage of this principle by writing down all the qualities you desire to develop?

7. The principle of auto-suggestion "will give you the surprise of your life and place you wherever you wish to be!" What surprise is waiting for you? Where do you want to be?

3

LIVING A
MILEAGE-
PLUS LIFE

Twelve Great Riches of Life are cited and explained in great detail in my book *Think and Grow Rich*. One of those great riches is *the habit of going the extra mile*. May I say that I never knew anyone to achieve outstanding success in any calling without strictly following the habit.

The habit of going the extra mile means providing *more* service and *better* service than what we are paid for and doing so with a pleasant mental attitude—without being requested to do so.

Most people do not have this habit—so those who do stand out to employers and to potential buyers as well. To be exact, only about two out of every one hundred people offer this sort of service—and they are the ones who are successful. The other ninety-eight are engaged in trying to get something for nothing. They are not willing to go the first mile, let alone the second mile.

VALUABLE BENEFITS

Going the extra mile—doing more than asked or required—provides more benefits than you can even imagine. Some of the more important benefits of going the extra mile include:

- Attracts favorable attention to you of people who can and do provide advancement and sales opportunities.

- Permits you to become indispensable in many different human relationships.

- Enables you to command more than the average compensation.

- Leads to mental growth and physical perfection in various forms of service, thereby developing greater ability and skill in your chosen vocation.

- Protects you against the loss of employment.

- Places you in a position to choose your own job and working conditions.

- Attracts self-promotion opportunities.

- Enables you to profit by the law of contrast. The vast majority of people don't do more than they have to—they actually try to get more than they are entitled to. So anyone who puts forth more-than-average effort stands out from the others and will be acknowledged.

MORE
VALUABLE BENEFITS

Other benefits to going the extra mile:

- Leads to the development of a positive, pleasing mental attitude, which is among the more important traits of a successful career and life.

- Develops a keen, alert imagination, as it is a habit that keeps you continuously seeking new and more efficient ways of rendering useful service for and to others.

- Develops the important factor of personal initiative to acquire economic freedom; avoiding mediocrity. Personal initiative is the most outstanding trait of the typical successful American citizen. Ours is a nation literally built on personal initiative.

- Develops self-reliance.

- Develops the confidence others have in your integrity and general abilities.

- Aids you in mastering the destructive habit of procrastination, which is among the more common causes of failure in all walks of life.

- Develops definiteness of purpose, without which there is no hope for success.

- Makes easy application of the master mind principle through which personal power is attained, and gives you the right to ask for promotion and more pay—and more sales.

EXTRA-MILE SUCCESS STORY

I observed from the personal analysis of more than 30,000 successful men and women who followed this principle— and the failures who did not. During my association with the late Andrew Carnegie, he called this principle to my attention as being a must for all who wish to get ahead in life. He said it was strict application of the going the extra mile principle by his highest paid employee, Mr. Charles M. Schwab, which promoted Mr. Schwab from a job as day laborer earning $25 a month to an executive position at $75,000 a year.

Then Mr. Carnegie shocked me by saying that in addition to the $75,000 annual salary, he sometimes paid Mr. Schwab as much as $1 million a year extra as a bonus because of the example he set for the other employees by his habit of going the extra mile. In other words, Mr.

Carnegie paid Mr. Schwab more than ten times as much for doing more than he was required to do.

Mr. Carnegie inspired every worker in his huge steel industry to follow Mr. Schwab's example, and many of them did so—and they became immensely wealthy.

EVEN NATURE CONFIRMS

Nature herself gives you proof that going the extra mile is sound and logical. The whole of the entire system of the universe, from this little earth on which we live to the largest stars, is an endorsement of this principle.

Let's take a look into nature's ways. Nature goes the extra mile by producing enough of everything for her needs together with an over-production for emergencies and waste. Fruit on the trees, frogs in the pond, fish in the seas, nature produces enough to ensure perpetuation of all species of every living thing, allowing for emergencies of every sort.

And nature has arranged for all her creatures to be adequately compensated for all they do in carrying out her plans. Bees are provided with honey as compensation for their service in fertilizing the flowers. But mind you they have to perform the service to get the honey, and it must be performed in advance.

Go the extra mile by providing better service than what you are paid for.

After the farmer has done his part for his labor and intelligence in planting and attending his crops, nature compensates the farmer. Nature yields him not only the original seed that he planted, but an over-flush in the form of compensation, thus giving him the benefit of the law of action and reaction.

Throughout the universe, everything has been so arranged through the law of compensation so adequately described by poet Ralph Waldo Emerson that nature's budget is always balanced always, so to speak. Everything has it's opposite equivalent in something else, positive and negative in every unit of energy, day and night, hot and cold, darkness and light, summer and winter, good and bad, up and down, success and failure, sweet and sour, happiness and misery, man and woman.

Everywhere and in everything, we can see the law of action and reaction in operation throughout nature. The pendulum swings back the same distance that it swings forward, the same in human relationships in rendering personal service as in all other endeavors.

TEST THE RULE

You can put it down as an established fact that if you neglect to develop and apply the principle of going the extra mile, you will never become personally successful—and you will never become financially independent. This is borne out by the fact that all successful people, especially in the higher brackets of success, follow this habit as an established part of their daily routine in all their human relationships. Test any successful person by this rule and be convinced.

Observe any person who is not a success and also be convinced.

We must render as much service as we are being paid for to hold a job or maintain a source of income, whatever it may be. But we also have the privilege always of providing an extra amount of service as a means of accumulating a reserve credit of good will and as a means of gaining higher pay and a better position. If no such surplus is rendered, we have no argument in favor of asking for a better position or increased pay. Think this over for yourself and you will have the real answer as to why it pays to give more and better service than you are being paid for.

Every position provides us with an opportunity to apply this principle, and in this very fact consists the major benefit of the great American system of free enterprise, which has made this the richest and freest nation on earth. To preserve this principle of free enterprise—based on the privilege of individual self-determination—that World War II was waged at such great expense.

May I add that the human imagination is not sufficient to produce a single sound argument against the use of the principle of going the extra mile. The person who says, "I'm not paid to do this or that. Therefore I'll not do it," simply writes himself an insurance policy for failure.

Render more service and better service than you are paid for, and provide it willingly with a positive mental attitude—then write yourself an insurance policy for success. The rule has never failed to work and it never will.

Last but not least, remember that the positive mental attitude is the factor that determines more than all else during the time between the delivery of the service or sale, and the pay off.

FAR-FLUNG SUCCESS

The following thrilling story is of a man who flew 7,000 miles to confer on personal and business matters. Every week on a radio program, men and women who have applied this philosophy in a practical manner to obtain fame and fortune for themselves and to bring great riches to others, would tell their stories. They participated of their own free will and entirely without compensation—except the compensation from telling others of the good things discovered along life's pathway.

One such businessman was from far off Bombay, India. He is head of the Modern Trading Corporation, the exclusive representative in India for a number of manufacturers in England, Switzerland, France, Canada, and the United States. It also represents many technical publications and trade papers in the Dominion of Canada. A portion of his interview follows:

> My country represents one of the very oldest civilizations on the face of the earth and your country is one of the very youngest. You had an old civilization before Columbus discovered America, and after seeing some of your customs I am glad the colonist discovered America instead of India, the country for which he was searching.
>
> It was 1937 when *Think and Grow Rich* was first published. A friend of mine who knew my interest in such things loaned me his copy of the first American edition of Dr. Hill's book. I found it so enlightening and so sound that I read every one of his books, including the *Law of Success*. I have studied Napoleon Hill's philosophy for the last eight years.
>
> Napoleon Hill's philosophy has helped me to clear my mind of wrong emotions, it has helped to eliminate waste of time and given me a clear understanding, enabling me to put

Nothing succeeds faster than honesty, truth, and frankness.

my knowledge to work with honesty of purpose and fairness with everybody. With these things accomplished, real success is possible.

In following Napoleon Hill's principles, I have obtained a respected place amongst my fellow people. I have gained the friendship of those with high principles. I have developed a distinctive character of reliability and dependability, which is a necessary preparedness for the way to riches to come.

His teachings enable me to apply the master mind principle. This in turn enables me to have the highest cooperation from the largest number of people, because nothing succeeds faster than honesty, truth, and frankness.

I imagine the notion to become rich is one that can enter any human mind, but to know the correct laws and to be prepared to go up the hill regardless of the difficulties is something that requires more than just a notion. I realize that achievement requires a great amount of labor but I'm prepared for that, and I'm armed with the right principles.

I am also fully prepared to make the right application of these principles in my search for the truth. To me, Napoleon Hill is a light house and which I shall continue to follow until a man is born who writes better and nobler than Dr. Hill has done. And, I shall look forward to discussing with Napoleon Hill how to make his noble and beneficial philosophy available to all of India. It is my desire to introduce Dr. Hill to a great philosopher, Mr. Gandi.

This man from Bombay, India lives every moment of his existence by the principles of success you are learning in this book. His understanding of the philosophy is such that he has been able to negotiate a great amount of business for his firm in Europe and in the United States. Before he returns to his native India, in a matter of weeks he expects the amount of business contracted for him to exceed $1 million, and he estimates that within the next two or three years the profits of his concern will run into millions of dollars each year.

This is an imposing tribute to the philosophy that you too can take advantage of. This interview—and many others similar—proves that no matter where you live, it is possible to take the philosophy of individual achievement and use it to *Think and Grow Rich*.

POINTS TO PONDER

1. "The habit of going the extra mile means providing *more* service and *better* service than what we are paid for and doing so with a pleasant mental attitude—without being requested to do so." Considering your line of work, describe what going the extra mile would look like on a daily basis. A weekly basis.

2. What is the best-case scenario you can expect if you choose to go above and beyond what is necessary to "get by" in life?

3. Of the 13 valuable benefits this extra-mile principle provides, which 5 would be the most impactful, most life-changing?

4. "The rest of the story" of Charles M. Schwab: At 35 years old, he was named president of the Carnegie Steel Corporation, and in the year 1900 profits reached $40 million. At age 38 when Carnegie sold his steel company, Schwab received $24 million worth of bonds (about $800 million in 2021 dollars). And at 39 he became president of the world's first billion-dollar corporation.[1] His rise to riches

began when someone saw his lifestyle of going the extra mile. What heights can you imagine for yourself by adopting this principle?

5. What other examples in nature can you list where the extra mile is evident?

6. Who comes immediately to mind when thinking of someone who does just enough to get by, who lives from paycheck to paycheck? Who comes immediately to mind when thinking of someone who goes above and beyond at work, play, in relationships, etc.

7. Compare the attitudes, demeanors, and lifestyles of the two people who came to mind.

NOTE

1. Gary Hoover, "Forgotten Business Giant: Charles M. Schwab," *American Business History Center*, February 26, 2021; https:// americanbusinesshistory.org/forgotten-business-giant-charles-m -schwab/; accessed September 13, 2023.

4

UNDERSTANDING YOURSELF AND OTHERS

In my book *The Master Key to Riches*, I describe another of the Twelve Great Riches of Life—the capacity to understand people, which is an ability everyone can acquire. This necessary ability affects all aspects of our lives including our career, relationships, lifestyle, joy, and our successes or failures.

The first step toward understanding others is to learn to understand yourself, for it is true that underneath the skin and in the workings of the mind we are all very closely akin.

If we can't understand others, we've not learned to understand ourselves. To understand others, we must make up our minds to accept them as they are, not as we wish them to be. I believe here is where the majority of people fail in their ability to understand people. They are more concerned with *changing* others to fit their own notions, than they are in *understanding* them.

Also, in order to understand people, we must learn to recognize both their good and bad traits. We must realize that no one is perfect, that no two people are exactly alike, that everybody is expressing his or her vision of life as they see it—and that *everyone has a motive* for everything they do, although maybe not always a sound motive.

We must also recognize that all people are what they are because of three great forces:

1. Physical heredity (sound physical health)

2. Social heredity (sound social and cultural health)

3. Law of cosmic habit force, which fixes all habits (definiteness of action, patterns of thoughts)

How many such motives govern people's lives? There are nine basic motives, some combination of which is responsible for every act. Before we gain the capacity to understand people, we must recognize these basic motives:

1. Emotion of love

2. Emotion of sex

3. Desire for financial or material gain

4. Desire for self-preservation

5. Desire for freedom of body and mind

6. Desire for personal expression and recognition from others

7. Desire for immortality or life after death

8. Desire for revenge for real or imaginary grievances

9. Emotion of fear

There are seven major fears:

1. Fear of poverty

2. Fear of criticism

3. Fear of ill health

4. Fear of loss of love

5. Fear of loss of liberty

6. Fear of old age

7. Fear of death

When you understand these nine basic motives, you will have gone a long way toward understanding the actions of all of humankind—both the good and the bad.

ADVERSITY

One of the greatest of all the influences that gives us the capacity to understand others is the experience of

To understand others, we must accept them for who they are.

adversity—failure, defeat. It is a known truth that any great sorrow alerts the human soul to recognize the true nature of the character of others and to know themselves as well. And, it is known that every adversity carries with it the seed of an equivalent benefit. *When any adversity strikes us, there is a blessing to be found in it as great as the adversity itself!*

This recognition of the true character of others through some experience of adversity often constitutes that seed of an equivalent benefit. Let me give you a few examples of what I mean, Abraham Lincoln, the Great Emancipator, found himself and developed the capacity to understand others through the greatest romantic adversity of his life, the death of the only woman he truly loved, Ann Rutledge.

Before this great tragedy overtook him, Lincoln was merely a nobody from nowhere, who had failed at every-thing he undertook. He took up surveying, but the sheriff sold his instruments for his debts. He tried store keeping and failed at that too. He joined the Army and went away with a company of soldiers as their captain, but he was soon demoted to a private. He took a turn at practicing law, but made no great reputation in this field of endeavor. Then adversity struck deeply into the soul of that great man and revealed in him the man whom this nation needed to carry it through its greatest crisis. Remember these facts concerning Abraham Lincoln and you will know how he developed so great a capacity to understand others.

Another example is John Bunyan who wrote *The Pilgrim's Progress*, one of the greatest works of literature of its kind. He wrote it while suffering the humiliation and hardship of prison, where he was confined because of his religious beliefs. With this book written in prison, he wrote himself a ticket to fame for all time.

Adversity is nothing to be afraid of, it not only reveals the true nature of the person who experiences it, but it also provides the individual with the capacity to understand other people just as they are.

Take the case of the farmer Milo C. Jones, in Fort Atkinson, Wisconsin, for example. He barely made a living from his farm until he was overtaken by adversity. He was stricken with double paralysis. Being thus deprived of the use of his body, he made the greatest of all discoveries. He discovered he had a brain, which was still intact, and it had the power to bring him the seed of an equivalent benefit to compensate for the loss of the use of his body.

He went to work with that brain and in a matter of days came up with an idea that made him a multimillionaire. Moreover, he made his fortune from the same farm from which he had barely been making a living before his adversity. He converted the farm into the raising of corn, and started raising pigs which he fed with his corn. The pigs he converted into the now famous Little Pig Sausage, which he sold across the nation. You see, adversity is a great developer of ideas, and it often leads to self-discovery through which we discover the genius that lies sleeping within our own dormant minds.

Through the adversity of deafness, the great Thomas A. Edison discovered the means of listening from within, through the use of his sixth sense. And by his development through the use of his sixth sense, he became the greatest inventor of all times, even though he had little formal schooling.

Let us remember that nearly all people hit bottom in some form of failure or defeat before they begin to climb high up the ladder of success. I have observed by studying successful people, that their measure of success always is in exact proportion to their experiences of previous failure or defeat.

A BLESSING
IN DISGUISE

Generally speaking, failure is a blessing in disguise. The effect that failure or defeat has on any person depends upon that person's reaction to the experience. For example, Mr. Edison failed ten thousand times before he perfected the incandescent electric lamp. He once told me that he would have spent the remainder of his life on that one invention alone if he had not sooner found the secret of it.

This is the sort of reaction to failure that makes it a blessing instead of a curse. It is the sort of reaction that the students of my philosophy are experiencing worldwide, and this accounts for their success, as they are reporting daily.

People of the South following the American War Between the States (the Civil War) accepted their loss of slaves as a failure. Their negative reaction to failure kept the South in economic bondage for many decades. Now the South has developed a new mental attitude toward this formerly perceived adversity and is promoting training and education for all, and this new attitude is giving it a new birth of economic freedom.

Let us remember that the mind attracts the physical counterpart of what it dwells on. People who go all the way through life with their minds fixed on the things they do not want, such as poverty, misery, ill health, and unhappiness, get these very things. But people with positive goals and determination, like automaker Henry Ford for example, fix their minds on what they desire and lo! they acquire it in an overabundance.

SUCCESS IS...

Success is the capacity to take full possession of your own mind and direct it toward the attainment of complete freedom of body and mind without violating the rights of others. May I add that this objective is the major purpose of my philosophy of success, and not only does this philosophy keep us from violating the rights of others, it enables us to pass on to others the greatest benefit.

And what is that greatest benefit? Helping others to help themselves by revealing the power gained by controlling their own mind. I fancy that if the devil ever shudders with fear, it is when he sees people taking full possession of their mind.

Some people have credited this philosophy for creating more successful men and women than any other. This is an astounding feat. The result of my philosophy was inspired by the great steel magnate Andrew Carnegie and organized with the help of more than 500 top-ranking men who have made this the greatest country on earth. They include Thomas A. Edison, Henry Ford, Charles M. Schwab, Frank A. Vanderlip, Dr. Alexander Graham Bell, Dr. Elmer R. Gates, and Colonel Edwin C. Barnes.

And let me not neglect to mention the greatest woman I have ever known, my own step-mother, who made it possible for me to publish these success principles in nearly two-thirds of the world and to inspire many millions of men and women to take possession of their own minds. My step-mother introduced me to my real self, that other self who knows no such realty as failure, and she inspired me to take possession of that self and make the fullest use of it.

I have found from experience that anyone can have anything they desire if they want it badly enough. What do I mean by badly enough? I mean that they must be willing to pay the just price for what they want and to keep their mind on it until they get it, no matter how long that may require.

For example, when Andrew Carnegie commissioned me to become the author of the world's first philosophy of individual achievement, I hardly knew the meaning of the word philosophy, but I wished to justify Mr. Carnegie's faith in me more than anything in the world. I was willing to devote 20 years of my life to the effort without immediate monetary compensation.

DEFINING SUCCESS

Am I successful? Here is my list of assets, and I'll leave it to the judgment of you as to whether or not I am a success. First of all, I have peace of mind, which means happiness. I have an abundance of the entire Twelve Great Riches of Life, including money, which is what I suspect most people ask about. I have sound physical health and I have a

The mind attracts the physical counterpart of what it dwells on.

wonderful wife who helps me serve the people through my philosophy, and with whom I am thoroughly in accord.

I work when I please and I play when I please. I hate no one and no one is my enemy, as far as I'm concerned. I have no fear of anything or of anyone. I have no unfulfilled desires of any nature whatsoever, and I have the privilege of taking to the world a philosophy that the greatest thinkers of the world believe to be the solution of the world's aliments. Through this philosophy I have benefited millions of people and eventually I hope to benefit many more millions.

I go to bed when I please and get up when I please. I can live in any portion of the world that I please, and I choose to live in California, the garden spot of the United States. If this is not success, then I shall be glad to have someone tell me what else I need to make my success complete.

Finally, to this end of helping others acquire what they desire, my entire life is dedicated. I hope this answers the question properly about my success.

SUCCESSFUL INTERVIEW

One day a radio interview included a man who was well known not only up and down the Pacific Coast, but all across the nation, as an expert in physical culture. Many businessmen in Los Angeles, pressed for time but realizing the benefits of a strong, healthy body depend on the Williams Health Service to keep them fit. The following is what Mr. V.C. Williams, had to say about this philosophy you have been reading about.

When *Think and Grow Rich* was first published, things were tight and I was looking for help. I learned about some fellow who was studying Napoleon Hill's new book, so about thirty or forty of us got together and met each week to read and study this book.

The book was stimulating and inspiring, and it gave us all courage to do the things we wanted to do at a time when courage was limited. In 1937, everybody seemed to be having a bit of a rough time. So, we'd meet every week and read Napoleon Hill's great book *Think and Grow Rich,* and we'd study it and try to apply its teachings to each one of our own problems.

I remember those master mind groups with great pleasure. We all made friendships that have lasted through the years. I am sure every man's success was increased many times as a direct result of our study of Napoleon Hill's book.

There are too many people who study a philosophy and think it's just something to study and make you feel good. Our group never for a moment thought of Napoleon Hill's writings as something to study and smile over and do nothing. We recognized that there were rules for success that any man, every man, could take and use. I used to think business was a struggle in which some men just won, because they were destined to win, and some lost because they were supposed to lose, but that isn't so.

Men win because they have a road map like the philosophy of Napoleon Hill. They win because they use the principles of success as outlined by Napoleon Hill in his books. As far as I am concerned, I think Dr. Hill's rules for success are so clear, so logical, so sensible and so necessary that I honestly believe no man can achieve success unless he does use them. They must be used, not just studied.

I think the one sentence that tells this story best is this. *Do something about it.* Don't just read and smile, do something, do anything that occurs to you, do something every day, don't expect any magic. Read one paragraph in Napoleon Hill's book, then do what it tells you. Then read another paragraph, then do something else. Eventually you will be doing everything he tells you to do, and then you can't help but be successful. By that time, you will really have learned how to *Think and Grow Rich* with Napoleon Hill.

The philosophy and principles you have been reading about are all proven successful for millions of people. People from all walks of life including salespeople, laborers, business owners, pilots, farmers, healthcare workers, teachers, even volunteers. Whether selling services or products or yourself in service to others, having these nuts and bolts in your toolbelt will in the long run hold together a lifestyle of success and satisfaction.

POINTS TO PONDER

1. On a scale from 1 (not good) to 10 (very good), how would you rate yourself regarding understanding yourself? _____

   a. On that same scale, how would you rate yourself regarding understanding other people? _____

    b. What steps will you take to improve your capacity to understand yourself?

    c. To understand others?

2. Are you more concerned with *changing others* to fit your own notions, than you are in *understanding* them?

3. Of the nine basic motives that govern people's lives, which two most influence you? Which two are the least influential in your life?

4. Of the seven fears that affect all people, which one is at the top of your list? Now list the remaining six in the order of your most fearful to the least. Can you identify reasons for each fear?

5. What are the differences between failure, defeat, and adversity? What are the similarities?

6. Can you identify with the phrase that failures are blessings in disguise? Do you believe it? How many times are you willing to fail before giving up?

7. After reading the author's definition of his
   success, how close are you to being able
   to list those same aspects of that lifestyle?
   _____ How many will you be able to
   list five years from now? _____ Ten
   years? _____

5

HARMONIOUS
HEALTH

As mentioned previously, in my book *The Master Key to Riches,* I describe the Twelve Great Riches of Life. One of those riches is *harmony in human relationships,* which means the art of getting along with people without friction.

As with the previous chapter about Understanding Yourself and Others, this chapter emphasis the critical and necessary ability to harmonize with others to bring out the best in them—and you, bringing success in every aspect of your life.

Let's say you have made up your mind to learn the art of relating to others in the spirit of harmony. How and where do you start?

I may as well begin right here with a brief lesson on acquiring this art. First of all, let me tell you that friction in machinery costs hundreds of millions of dollars annually, but any intelligent worker can tell you that this is mere chicken feed when compared with the cost of friction between the people who handle the machinery—including everyone connected with the machine, from the top management down to the humblest worker.

This lesson applies to any and every business, corporation, and organization, including sales, education, entertainment, sports, media, etc.

Let's begin by laying out a program for mastering friction in human relationships that will result in closing that sale, landing that job, and/or making that team.

A POSITIVE MENTAL ATTITUDE

The very first step is to develop and maintain one of the Twelve Great Riches of Life—a positive mental attitude.

The reason? Your own mental attitude is picked up by everyone around you, although you may not open your mouth or even make a move indicating what is in your mind. If your mental attitude is negative and is filled with anger or worry or dislike for someone, whoever is around you will pick up that attitude and hand it right back to you as their attitude toward you.

So you see how you cannot hope to establish harmony in your relations with those near you unless you feel right toward them and keep your mind free from negatives, every negative.

SHARE YOUR BLESSINGS

Next, to establish harmony in your relations with others, you must be willing to share your blessings with them. A selfish person does not attract harmony. You will recall that the habit of going the extra mile is one of the Twelve Great Riches of Life. The person who follows this habit finds it easier to attract harmonious cooperation from others. Nature has a law known as the law of harmonious attraction, meaning that *like attracts like* in all relation-ships. Whatever thoughts you send out from your mind come back greatly multiplied by a flock of their relatives. "Whatsoever a man soweth that shall he also reap" is not merely a biblical statement, it is an essential principle of a sound success philosophy.

Know too that the art of harmony in human relation-ships has a definite price tag attached to it.

But the price is well within the reach of everyone who desires this great asset. Let us not forget that harmony in human relations cannot be attained without a sincere level of respect and affection for people, all people.

Dogs know instinctively when people like them or dis-like them. They definitely indicate it by a reciprocation of whichever state of mind they detect. Wild animals have the same instinct. Humans have it too but seldom make use of it. That is one reason why I wrote the *Master Key to Riches*, to alert people as to *how to get along with other people.*

Getting along with people goes deeper than mere words and deeds. This deepness consists in the mental attitude you hold, the thoughts that dominate your mind. We can easily cut out the very foundation of success from under ourselves without doing or saying anything to offend others.

"Whatsoever a man soweth, that shall he also reap."

—Galatians 6:7, The Bible

Let me give you an example of what I mean. I was retained by the R.G. LeTourneau Company to eliminate friction among its employees and to positivize their minds for relationships governed by harmony. When I began my work, I was literally deluged with complaints from the employees, often receiving as many as fifty in one day. Analysis showed that most of these were petty or without a definite cause. Within six months all complaints from the employees had been eliminated, for I had shown them a better way of getting what they desired through friendly, harmonious cooperation carried out by going the extra mile.

BUILDING HARMONY

There was one factor that entered into this case that was critically important—I related myself to the employees in a spirit of brotherly love, for my job was truly a labor of love. I never listened to a complaint from an employee that I did not mentally change places with him or her, seeing myself sitting in the chair where the employee sat. This attitude builds harmony no matter what the human relationship may be.

I have seen employees come in with snarls on their lips and go out with smiles on their faces and feelings of gratitude in their hearts—even if they did not get what they came after. They received something much greater, a changed mental attitude. I believe this is what most people in the world need today, *a changed mental attitude.*

A man came to see me a few weeks ago with a very serious personal problem. He began his story this way: "I am forty-eight years old, I have a college education, and I am rated as a first class accountant. I do my work efficiently, I tend to my own business and never interfere in the affairs of others—but despite all of this, I am being constantly persecuted by others. They often go out of their way to make my work difficult, and sometimes they cause me to leave my job. What is wrong with people anyway?"

After two hours of questioning, I learned from this man what was really wrong. It was not with other people, it was with himself. He was right in saying that people often went out of their way to persecute him, but he overlooked the reason for this. The reason was his mental attitude toward people. He believed himself superior to others and plainly indicated this in his mental attitude toward them. He resented the so-called tormentors and did not hesitate to show his resentment by striking back with words expressing hatred. *You cannot hate people and expect them to love you.*

I sent this man away with a formula for maintaining harmony in human relations. Here is the gist of it just as I gave it to him:

One, go the extra mile.

Two, become humble in your own heart.

Three, share your blessings with others.

Four, learn to like people as they are.

Five, smile at people when you speak to them.

You may be surprised to know that those five simple rules gave my client a changed mental attitude. Only a few days ago, he came to see me a second time—to tell me how proud he was to have learned that the cause of his previous friction with people had been walking around under his own hat, without him knowing it was there.

Every person who fails may see the person who caused that failure, by looking into the mirror.

Generally speaking, *the person who fails does so because of pride*. Successful people have learned how to trade pride for humility. Pride often inspires opposition from others. Humility of the heart inspires friendly cooperation.

Many people associate disgrace with failure. If there really was disgrace associated with failure, Thomas Edison would have been disgraced beyond hope of redemption every time he failed in his attempt to invent the incandescent electric light.

I believe if people understood that failure is only the absence of success, it may help them overcome it. Whoever you are, wherever you may be, *if you wish to establish harmony in your relations with others, clear your mind of all resentment, all pride, all envy, and all hatred—and develop a way to share your blessings with as many as will receive them.* Then watch how quickly every circumstance of your life will change for the better. Don't take my word for it. Just try it and be convinced.

HOME SWEET HOME LIFE

Not long ago I had as a client a man who was troubled by a lack of harmony with his wife. I gave him explicit instructions as to how he should proceed, and ended up by suggesting that he go past the flower shop and purchase a nice bouquet for his wife and take along also a nice box of candy, just to show his change of mental attitude toward her.

As soon as he presented her with those gifts, she promptly called me on the telephone to check and make sure he had been at my office.

Did the gifts really upset her that much? Yes, indeed, they did. You see, he had not shown her that sort of courtesy for a long while, and naturally she was suspicious as to the cause of his sudden change of heart. I suspect she thought his gifts were motivated by some mischief that he had been up to. But it turned out all right as I explained that I had been the author of the gift idea, and that she might expect more gifts in the same spirit in which her husband brought these home.

The small privileges, the kindly spoken words, the smile on the lips, the warm grasp of the hand shake that really convey our mental attitude. The alert person looks for these little signs that occur innocently and disclose what takes place in the mind. On the other hand, a so-called wise crack or a bit of so-called friendly sarcasm expressed by anyone may result in the loss of a friendship, a loved one, a job, a sale, a promotion, etc.

Most marriages that break up do not do so in one fell swoop. They break up little by little through a wrong tone of voice, sharp words, and a negative mental attitude expressed silently.

How fortunate it is that the way to harmonious human relations consists of many little steps that anyone can understand and use with ease. All the great truths are simple in the final analysis. If this were not so, then truth would be monopolized by a few. The road to personal success may not always be a short road, but it is clearly marked; and all who follow the road signs will arrive safely at their chosen destination.

May I add that there has never been an age of greater opportunity for personal achievement than the one in which we are now living. There is a market for every person's talents, no matter how humble they are, and plenty of money to pay for it. Despite all of these facts, there is confusion and chaos among the people because too few have a sound philosophy of life by which to guide themselves.

If I had to condense my advice regarding harmonious human relations into one sentence, I would say, *"Harmony can be achieved by honesty of purpose and just plain sincerity based on a keen sense of justice."* It is easy to get along with people when you have a sincere desire to be fair with people. This kind of mental attitude always inspires reciprocation in the same attitude. So you see the business of creating harmony in human relations is something every person can sow if they so desire.

It's been said that that when a person is ready for anything, it is always attracted to that person; likewise, when the student is ready the teacher appears. I've seen this philosophy demonstrated hundreds of times. As a matter of fact, my first service to a new student of my philosophy is to condition the person's mind so he's ready for whatever he most desires in life.

The following interview is with a successful businessman and illustrates the power and importance of the principles of success you have read throughout the book:

Do whatever you do with the right mental attitude.

Mr. M. J. Benjamin, head of the M.J. Benjamin Orthopedic Appliance Company in the Paramount Building in downtown Los Angeles is well known to many. He is a member of the Los Angeles Breakfast Club, was president of the Rotarians and is past president of the Cooperators Club. He shares:

With a success philosophy you have a road map which shows you just how to get through life's detours, or even how to avoid them. A person without a philosophy just slouches along in the mud and rain and has no way of knowing whether he will ever get through the detour or not.

I was left a small one-man business when my father passed on. He had developed it and gotten most of the wrinkles out of it, but suddenly I was the owner, manager, and only employee. If anyone ever needed a philosophy of life, I did. It doesn't make much difference what happens to us in this world; it's our reaction to life's events that really counts.

Naturally I felt quite alone in this world. My father had been the guiding light and I of course had depended on him. I did not inherit any financial means, so I was required to concentrate on building a successful business.

I decided to do the best I knew, and to keep doing better and more work than I was expected to do. Even then I seemed to recognize that this was the thing to do, and so that's what I did.

And it worked. It always works. It's a law and infallible rule. It's just as sure as night and day. I discovered this one rule about going the extra mile for myself, and I discovered some other rules, but I naturally didn't uncover all the rules for success, as Dr. Hill has done. That just proves that young men and women today have much greater advantages than I had because they can read all the seventeen fundamentals of success and follow them without having to take decades to discover them as Napoleon Hill has done.

In other words, no matter what business they choose or follow, the rules for success will still prove to be a safe road map to whatever goal a person wishes to reach.

Life is so complicated today; we need calm, clear thinkers like Napoleon Hill to guide us and inspire us and verify our own philosophy. While we're on the subject, I'd like to say that Dr. Hill's philosophy is not a philosophy based on greed and money grabbing. Money is an important tool in the world of today. Napoleon Hill's philosophy is a practical philosophy and it deals in money, and lots of it, but it doesn't neglect the other riches of life. It's truly an inspired philosophy that the world needs badly.

A friend gave me a copy of *Think and Grow Rich* soon after it was published. It fit into my own belief system so perfectly that I have been a student and a follower of Napoleon Hill ever since. In fact, I'll go further than that and say that all of my success is due to the application of the success principles taught by Napoleon Hill—takes in a lot of territory.

Every day of my life I see men better equipped than I with education and natural ability. I see bigger men and men with greater potentiality who have missed success for just one reason—they have not organized their personal power according to the philosophy and success rules of Napoleon Hill.

I have recommended Napoleon Hill's books to everyone I meet, and here on the radio this afternoon I again recommend them to all who wish to know the rules for business and personal success.

In twenty-seven years, my organization has grown from a one-man business to today occupying ten rooms and employing more than twenty people. More than 50,000 people in Southern California are familiar with our corrective and orthopedic appliances because they were recommended by their physicians and surgeons.

The one factor in Napoleon Hill's philosophy that has been more responsible for my success than any other is his principle of going the extra mile. That is the one, more than all the others. That's described by Dr. Hill as *doing more and better work than you're paid to do and doing it all the time and in a positive mental attitude.*

The part in this principle that most people overlook is the importance of doing what you do in the right mental attitude. That's the part that brings us some of life's greatest riches. Mr. Benjamin certainly has enjoyed in abundance one of the greatest riches of life. He has done so by manufacturing aids to a healthy use of a body, thus assisting people to lead nearly normal lives. Most surely that can be classed as a labor of love.

For those new or not too familiar with the Philosophy of American Achievement, let us enumerate some of the benefits it has brought to various people. It has snatched unhappy, despondent individuals from the very edge of failure and has given hope and direction to their lives. It has restored harmony to countless disorganized homes, cheating the divorce courts time and time again. It has developed confidence in defeated men, spurring them on to a fuller use of their unlimited powers.

It has helped men and women market useful ideas that lay dormant and useless for years. It has assisted people to obtain financial backing for worthy projects, ideas, and businesses. It has brought harmony and peace to management and labor in many organizations.

The personal fortunes it has helped to create are almost beyond comprehension. Wherever and whenever these success formulas are applied, people are happier, richer, more useful citizens of their community and marketplace.

POINTS TO PONDER

1. When reading about the friction in machinery costing hundreds of millions of dollars annually, did a closer-to-home scenario come to your mind? Is there friction between the people with whom you work that prevent a smooth operation, efficient production, or lucrative sales?

2. When handling an employee or buyer's questions or complaints, do you routinely mentally change places with him or her, seeing yourself in their shoes, so to speak? If you don't have this habit, how do you think it would change your attitude and response to the person?

3. Have you noticed someone's bad attitude even though there was no conversation between the two of you? What is a natural response to someone who is exhibiting a negative attitude?

4. "Pride often inspires opposition from others. Humility of the heart inspires friendly cooperation." How easy is it for you to exchange pride for humility in everyday situations?

5. "Failure is only the absence of success." What exactly does this statement mean to you? Does it sound more like an excuse, or a solid motivation?

6. Do you believe the statement, "There is a market for every person's talent and plenty of money to pay for it"?

7. How would you define the Philosophy of American Achievement and all its benefits?

How have you personally benefited from living in the United States?

6

UNFINISHED
BUSINESS

A look back in time...

Lying in my book shelves, not ten feet from where I sat, were the finished manuscripts of seven unpublished books, written while I was waiting for the Depression to wear itself out. They had never been offered to a publisher because I believed they were not good enough for publication. I knew, without doubt, however that any one of the manuscripts far surpassed the book I had just read. I knew also—and this was what most aggravated me—that a writer with a bunch of literary tripe had related herself to the publishers in such an effective manner that she had received a fortune for her efforts, while I was literally drifting to starvation, with a fortune in manuscripts gathering dust in my apartment.

But, that was not the entire cause of my embarrassment. I still had to pass the book over to my wife, and I well knew, before she even looked at it, that she would make the same comparisons between it and my own unpublished manuscripts. I wondered what her reaction would be when she discovered that I had been feeding her on short rations and forcing her to wear clothes she should have long since discarded, because I had drifted along without offering my books for publication. Frankly, the necessity of having to face her after she read the book I had just finished reading was one of the most embarrassing experiences since we had been married.

Finally my wife cleared away the dinner dishes and asked to see the book. I handed it to her and took a walk through Central Park to get some fresh air while she read it. I knew I would need the air after she discovered what I already knew. I gave her just enough time to finish the book, then sneaked back to the apartment.

My wife was pacing the floor and impatiently awaiting me. She did not give me time to say anything, but went straight to the point in a rapid fire analysis in which she unfavorably compared the book she had just read with one of my unpublished manuscripts, ending her analysis by saying, "What a joke this has been on us; working day and night for over a year, looking for a way for you to stage a comeback, counting pennies, picking newspapers out of ash cans—with a fortune in the house."

With that statement she made a dash for the book shelves, brought out one of the manuscripts and began to read it aloud! After she had finished reading about five pages of the manuscript she threw it all the way across the room with such speed that it smashed the floor lamp and destroyed the only light in the room, exclaiming as she did so, "Just think of that woman reaping a fortune for a book I am sure she could have written in two weeks, while you spent a quarter of a century gathering and organizing the material that went into this manuscript, yet you believe the book not good enough to go to the publisher!"

Her challenge was unanswerable except by my frank admission that she was right and I was just as disgusted as she. The next day we were still further humiliated when we learned that the writer of the book had sold the moving picture rights for a small fortune. The only thing the producer of the picture intended to use being the title, and incidentally that was all of the book that ever got into the picture, although it turned out to be a very profitable production.

A FORTUNE IN LITERARY ASSETS

We were so upset that we walked around town all night. We had entirely overlooked the importance of relating ourselves to the right people in the right way, as we could so easily have done if we had taken inventory of our literary assets before being forced to do so.

Before we knew it, we looked around and saw that dawn was breaking, so we walked across to the East River and stood on the bank while the sun rose. It was the most beautiful sunrise I had ever seen, and, as later events were destined soon to reveal, it was significant of the dawn of a new day—a new era—that was to shift us over from the negative side of the River of Life to the positive side.

Don't let your ideas and your work gather dust.

We went back to the apartment, had some breakfast, then went to bed and slept like two infants until late afternoon, for truly we had been newly born spiritually. After we were rested, we arose and went to work editing and rewriting the manuscript which, at that time, had been given the title of "The Thirteen Steps to Riches," but later was changed to *Think and Grow Rich*.

Before we were satisfied enough for the publisher to see the manuscript, we rewrote it three times (there were more than 300 typewritten pages), my wife doing the typing. By the time she had finished the manuscript on the third rewrite, the tips of her fingers were so worn and blistered she had to tape them so she could work, but she was so enthusiastic, because of the discovery we had made, that she said it was a pleasure to "wear her fingers to the bone" in such a labor of love.

We worked day and night, stopping for only enough time to get about four hours of sleep daily. We knew, after work on this book had been finished, how it was that the late Edison often managed to get along with four hours or less of sleep each day.

Finally the work was finished and our publisher was notified that the manuscript was ready for his inspection. He came in person to our apartment, inspected the manuscript quite quickly and cursorily, then spent the remainder of the day trying to explain why he did not believe the book would find a market.

We listened to his analysis but never opened our mouths until he had entirely relieved himself of his opinion concerning the book, because we knew before he ever saw the manuscript that he was going to publish it. We gave that matter no concern whatsoever, having already definitely made up our minds.

He had been talking all afternoon, analyzing the book and trying to prove to us it was not very different from other books he had published, none of which, he claimed, were selling at that time. "So why," he interrogated in his closing challenge, "do you believe this book would sell? What has it that is not in your other books I have published?"

I started to answer, but my wife took over the conversation and answered for me by suggesting that the publisher take the manuscript home with him, read it carefully, and then he would know what was in it that was not in my previous books, or any other book he had published.

That challenge brought the interview to an end. The publisher agreed that he had no right to pass judgment on the manuscript before reading it carefully, so he took it under his arm and departed. I remember so well what my wife said as he closed the door behind him: "He will publish that book, and that is not all; the book will make a place for itself, and be a best seller for years to come, whether he spends a nickel in advertising or not!"

Think and express your thoughts in terms of action.

To be agreeable I perfunctorily said, "Yes, my dear, I hope so!" To be truthful, I was not as sanguine as my wife over the fate of the book.

Three days later our publisher rushed in to our home, unannounced, with a smile on his face which seemed to us a mile wide. We knew, from the expression on his face, what sort of news he brought. He wanted a few minor changes made in the manuscript, after which he said it would go to press immediately, with instruction to push the book through as quickly as possible.

A few days later he wrote me a letter with one sentence I shall not soon forget. "I read the first two chapters of the book to my entire office force," he wrote, "and told them when I had finished that there were enough practical ideas in those two chapters alone to change the average person's life from failure to success." Subsequent events proved his words to have been more than the enthusiastic outburst of a hopeful publisher.

Two months later, the first edition came from the press and every copy was sold within three weeks, despite the fact that no publicity had been placed behind it other than circulars mailed by the publisher to some of his mail order book buyers. Then the book began to move over an ever-increasing territory, through one edition after another, until our financial worries vanished completely.

THINK AND TAKE ACTION

I am reminded now, as I think of my experience with the book that launched me off to a new start, that the major purpose of *Think and Grow Rich,* and for that matter all my other books, is to cause people to think and express their thoughts in terms of action. The book did all of that; therefore it served the highest purpose any book can serve.

And I have been abundantly blessed with cooperation from the minds of men and women intimately superior to my own, those who have added to the new interpretation of the Philosophy of American Achievement that vital spirit of unselfishness that has been responsible for the seeming miracles it is bringing into the lives of those who are following it.

If this were the last book I ever intended writing, and I desired to close it with the most beneficial thoughts within my power, I would say to you:

> *Set aside one hour out of ever twenty-four for silent meditation! For prayer if you wish to call it that.*
>
> *Get away to yourself, shut out all thoughts and desires associated with getting, and think only in terms of giving!*

Put aside all selfishness and think only of others!

Carry with you into your "silent hour" no thoughts of ownership of material things, and realize, as everyone should, that no one truly owns anything—only the privilege of thinking!

Open your mind to the guidance of whatever thoughts that may appear!

And come out with a firm determination that you will let no day pass without your having performed some act of useful service to others without any thought of material compensation.

Wars may bring temporary victory to one nation or another, through the force of arms, but the only enduring victory of real value that anyone may enjoy is the victory over self, a victory gained when we disavow all desire for material benefits at the expense of others, and embrace the more commendable desire to help others in the solution of the pressing problems of their daily lives.

When that victory is attained, all other needs will be added unto it; aided by the help of that mysterious power that comes from within!

Recognize the full meaning of this thought, and you will have acquired a peace of mind that "surpasses understanding"!

POINTS TO PONDER

1. Do you have unfinished business sitting on your shelf? Asleep in your filing cabinet? Lying in your tool box? Resting on your desk? Gathering dust in your workshop? Lying dormant in your closet? Bouncing around in your mind? What will it take to get that unfinished business onto your "take action" to-do list?

2. Have you been struck with seeing or hearing something and you knew deep down (without bragging) that you could do it better, say it better, or make it better? Why not take time to think about it and then do something about it, today!

3. What's holding you back from pursuing your dream? Achieving your goals? Reaching forward and/or upward to the next best level of living?

4. Do you have an "encourager" to motivate you into pushing yourself past your current comfort level? Think of someone who can forcefully urge to move beyond the status quo—into a new and exciting venture. Then contact that person, today!

5. Of the nine closing "beneficial thoughts," which three will you put into practice today?

6. Of the nine closing "beneficial thoughts," which three will you put into practice within the week?

7. Of the nine closing "beneficial thoughts," which will become lifetime habits—realizing that all will bring you everyday success, as well as eternal joy and contentment.

ABOUT NAPOLEON HILL

(1883-1970)

"Remember that your real wealth can be measured not by what you have — but by what you are."

In 1908, during a particularly down time in the U.S. economy and with no money and no work, Napoleon Hill took a job to write success stories about famous men. Although it would not provide much in the way of income, it offered Hill the opportunity to meet and profile the giants of industry and business—the first of whom was the creator of America's steel industry, multimillion-aire Andrew Carnegie, who became Hill's mentor.

Carnegie was so impressed by Hill's perceptive mind that following their three-hour interview he invited Hill to spend the weekend at his estate so they could continue the discussion. During the course of the next two days, Carnegie told Hill that he believed any person could achieve greatness if they understood the philosophy of success and the steps required to achieve it. "It's a shame," he said, "that each new generation must find the way to success by trial and error, when the principles are really clear-cut."

Carnegie went on to explain his theory that this knowledge could be gained by interviewing those who had achieved greatness and then compiling the information and research into a comprehensive set of principles. He believed that it would take at least twenty years, and that the result would be "the world's first philosophy of individual achievement." He offered Hill the challenge—for no more compensation than that Carnegie would make the necessary introductions and cover travel expenses.

It took Hill twenty-nine seconds to accept Carnegie's proposal. Carnegie told him afterward that had it taken him more than sixty seconds to make the decision he would have withdrawn the offer, for "a man who cannot reach a decision promptly, once he has all the necessary facts, cannot be depended upon to carry through any decision he may make."

It was through Napoleon Hill's unwavering dedication that his book, *Think and Grow Rich*, was written and more than 80 million copies have been sold.

THANK YOU FOR READING THIS BOOK!

If you found any of the information helpful, please take a few minutes and leave a review on the bookselling platform of your choice.

BONUS GIFT!

Don't forget to sign up to try our newsletter and grab your free personal development ebook here:

soundwisdom.com/classics

IF YOU ENJOYED
SELL YOUR VISION,

CHECK OUT THE
LIVE A LIFE THAT MATTERS SERIES.

Path to Purpose

7 Steps to
Living a Life that Matters

Achieving Your Goals

The Four Proven
Principles of Success

How to Create a
Motivated Mindset

Stay on the Path to Purpose
and Achieve Your Goals